DEALING WITH LOSS AND GRIEF

A RESOURCE FOR INTERMEDIATE/SENIOR TEACHERS

DEALING WITH LOSS AND GRIEF

A RESOURCE FOR INTERMEDIATE/SENIOR TEACHERS

Cathy Gross

Sharron McKeever

Mary Ann Takacs Debly

NOVALIS

Cover design and layout: Audrey Wells

Business Offices:
Novalis Publishing Inc.
10 Lower Spadina Avenue, Suite 400
Toronto, Ontario, Canada
M5V 2Z2

Novalis Publishing Inc.
4475 Frontenac Street
Montréal, Québec, Canada
H2H 2S2

Phone: 1-800-387-7164
Fax: 1-800-204-4140
E-mail: books@novalis.ca
www.novalis.ca

Library and Archives Canada Cataloguing in Publication

Gross, Cathy
    Dealing with loss and grief : a resource for intermediate/secondary
teachers / Cathy Gross, Sharron McKeever, Mary Ann Takacs Debly.

Includes bibliographical references.
ISBN-13: 978-2-89507-831-9
ISBN-10: 2-89507-831-9

    1. Grief in adolescence. 2. Loss (Psychology) in adolescence.
I. McKeever, Sharron   II. Takacs Debly, Mary Ann III. Title.

BF724.3.L66G76 2006   155.9'3   C2006-905808-3

Printed in Canada.

The Scripture quotations contained herein are from the New Revised Standard Version of the Bible, copyrighted 1989 by the Division of Christian Education of the National Council of the Churches of Christ in the United States of America, and are used by permission. All rights reserved.

We acknowledge the financial support of the Government of Canada through the Book Publishing Industry Development Program (BPIDP) for our publishing activities.

5 4 3 2 1   11 10 09 08 07

CONTENTS

Preface

Dear Teacher,

As educators, regardless of the role we play in the school community, we have the privileged vocation of helping to form our students. We journey with them through sunny days of joyful successes and stormy days of challenging difficulties. Some of our students struggle with losses in their lives. How can we support them during these painful times?

As teachers and Religion and Family Life Education consultants with 102 years of combined experience, we have had the honour of walking with and supporting students and staff as they wrestled with a wide range of life's losses. This resource is the fruit of our experiences and of the wisdom we gained over the years. We are pleased to share it with you.

Our hope is that the ideas we offer here will give you confidence and a sense of direction when you are called to support individuals, a class or the entire school community in times of loss or crisis. Perhaps the ideas in this resource will invite conversation and discussion in the staff room as well. You can't plan ahead for difficult events in the lives of your students or your school, but you can develop some insights and wisdom that will anchor you when dealing with loss.

All of us who lovingly embrace this ministry of accompanying others through loss are so blessed to have Jesus as our foundation – our guide. Jesus tells us, "I am the way, and the truth, and the life" (John 14:6). Jesus will never leave us; he stays with us in joy and in sorrow. As he reminds his disciples, "Remember, I am with you always, to the end of the age" (Matthew 28:20).

With our best wishes,

Cathy, Sharron and Mary Ann

I

An Introduction to Loss and Grief

This resource gives you the tools you need to support your students when they experience loss in their lives. It has been created to guide you as you assist students who are journeying through the grieving process, offer them hope, and eventually help them accept their loss with courage.

As much as you might want to, you cannot eliminate all pain and suffering from the lives of your students. By acknowledging Christ's presence even in the sadness and pain of loss, you provide students with meaning and hope. You do this by placing faith at the heart of the grieving process and by recognizing that Jesus always walks with us, even in life's darkest moments.

What is loss?

A loss is any personal sense of being deprived of something important. Feelings of loss are common to all of us, and each loss, whether it seems trivial or serious, has the potential to shape who we are and how we perceive ourselves in relationship to others. Our losses can have a profound effect that will extend across the whole of our lives.

Young people may experience some of the following losses.

Obvious Sources of Loss

- death of someone important (including miscarriage);

- loss of a pet (a pet that has died, run away or had to be given away for some reason);

- moving (or a close friend moving);

- changing schools;

- divorce;

- loss of friendship;

- breakup with a boyfriend or girlfriend;

- not fitting in;

- not being chosen for a team or group;

- loss of employment (parent or student);

- loss of home;

- theft;

- family events (chronic illness, grandparent moving in, new baby);

- an older sibling leaving for college, university or work.

Less Obvious Sources of Loss

- hospitalization;

- long periods of separation from a parent;

- bullying;

- being the subject of lies or gossip;

- abuse (sexual, physical, emotional);

- abortion;

- alcoholism in the family;

- humiliation (especially in front of peers);

- change of country or nationality;

- natural disasters;

- repeated failure;

- shattered fantasies (fallen heroes);

- rejection by university or college;

- failure to be hired for a job.

What is grief?

Grief is the name given to the myriad emotions we feel in response to loss. Grieving is a complex process of gradually integrating the loss we have endured and, ultimately, once again finding meaning and purpose in life. There is no one way to describe grief.

People experience a broad range of feelings after a loss. Some feel anger, guilt and alienation, while others feel hopelessness and despair. Not everyone will have the same quantity or intensity of feelings. Children in the same family may exhibit different emotions and respond in different ways to the same loss. As a teacher, allow your students to grieve in whatever way is best for them. At the same time, be aware that some kinds of behaviour can be harmful to the students themselves or to others. If you see this kind of behaviour, offer more intervention or seek professional help for the student (see Chapter 3).

The grieving process

Grieving is hard work. When life has been altered irrevocably, some-times it is all a person can do just to get out of bed in the morning and face a new day. Whatever the source of the loss – a divorce, a move, the loss of a friendship, or the death of a loved one (including that of a pet) – grieving involves a journey. No matter what age the grief-stricken person is, there are three main stages in grieving:

• confusion and shock;

• helplessness and despair; and

• acceptance and integration of the loss into life.

Emotional responses to loss do not necessarily follow this order. Very often a person will move back and forth from acceptance to confusion and despair. No one "gets over" a significant loss – but people can and do learn to live with their loss.

A major life loss, such as divorce, can take anywhere from a few years to a lifetime to become fully integrated in a person's life. In the griev-ing process, the immediate intense emotions eventually subside. It might seem that the worst pain is over. Then something can occur that triggers the intense feelings again. For example, a person who has gone through a divorce may find painful feelings resurfacing when supporting a close friend struggling with a marriage breakup. Over time, the intensity and frequency of these feelings do lessen. But they are never completely gone.

Throughout life, a single loss can continue to call up feelings of grief – not just for the loss itself, but also for the loss of all that might have been. For example, the loss of a parent is grieved immediately, because the person is gone from our presence at this moment in our life. As the years pass, precious moments that might have been shared with that parent are also experienced as loss, and grief is revisited. For young adults, these precious moments might include graduation, a first job, marriage or the birth of a child. They realize as these events occur that they have no father to share their successes, no grandfather to hug their grandchildren and sing them to sleep.

The aim of the grieving process is to allow people to move through the experience of loss and re-establish emotional energy into their lives. Healthy grieving results in a forward movement and making new connections in life. For example, after the loss of a friend, the process of grieving helps a person accept the finality of that loss and then move forward to build new friendships. If the grieving process cannot be completed in a healthy way, however, the grieving person may become withdrawn, afraid to make new friends for fear of further loss, and be unable to re-engage with life.

A healthy grieving process contains several essential components.

1. Accepting that the loss is real

When a loved one dies, we must accept that they cannot come back. After a divorce, family members need to acknowledge that they will not live together again. When a friend moves to another country, we must face the fact that we may fall out of touch. In each situation, as we grieve we must realize and accept that what we have lost cannot be retrieved; the separation is final. There is a division between life before the loss and the new reality that follows. Integrating this new reality takes time and is very painful, but it is essential for healthy grieving.

2. Experiencing the pain of the loss

The overwhelming pain and other feelings linked to loss are indispensable steps on the road to healing. Stuffing the feelings inside, running away from them or following other people's ideas of how we "should" feel only hinders the healing. Fortunate are we if we have someone who will listen to our story without judging, and who is strong enough to let us cry.

3. Adjusting to the changed environment

After a loss, life is now different. As we become aware of the changes in our lives, we may need to learn some new skills, such as finding fresh ways of doing things or relating to others. That growing aware-ness means we are beginning to be at home within the changed context of our life.

4. *Reinvesting emotional energy into other relationships or activities*

This difficult task requires that we integrate the experience of loss into our past understanding of life so that we can place our emotional energy into a new beginning. This turn to the future might feel like a betrayal, but accepting the loss does not mean we don't care. Rather, it means that we are ready to carry on, enriched by memories of persons, things and events that have formed us in the past and will continue to be a part of our lives in the future.

5. *Reconciling and forgiving*

If anger is involved in the loss, forgiveness and reconciliation may be necessary components of the grieving process. When moving forward after a divorce, for example, spouses may be angry at each other, or the children may be angry with one or both parents. When someone dies, we may be angry with that person for leaving us alone. Family members may be angry with a parent who accepts a job that requires all of them to move, disrupting friendships, school life and much more. Forgiveness and reconciliation can be a key part of a healthy grieving process. Even if we can never rekindle the relationship, let-ting go of bitterness, anger or the desire for revenge frees us to move on with our lives.

God is with us in our grief

When students question the actions or presence of God in their loss, it is important to communicate to them that loss is truly a mystery. God does not plan or desire their loss. God does not cause death or natural disasters. As Christians, the most important truth we can hold on to is that we know truly and unshakably that God is always with us. God loves us deeply and is present with us in our loss and in all the suffering it brings.

Turning to God at times of loss is very important, but at first, offering your thoughts about God may short-circuit a student's ability to begin grieving. People who are grieving must begin by getting in touch with their authentic feelings. A more appropriate time to begin discussing the presence of God as a source of peace, hope and new directions is after authentic feelings have been acknowledged and expressed.

As difficult as it may seem at the time of a painful loss, new life can come from the experience if we are patient and willing to open ourselves to new possibilities. We need to trust that God is right there with us and will stay with us as we work through the pain of the loss.

Conclusion

The journey of the grieving process is open-ended. There are no set timelines for expressing feelings and no one way to express them. Each person's grief journey is unique, just as the gift of each life is a unique and precious part of God's creation.

2

THE GRIEVING TEEN

As a teacher, you are one of the most influential adults in a teenage student's life. That is why it is important that you familiarize yourself with the ways loss and grief are experienced by students this age. If you know how teens commonly react to loss, you will be better able to support them with compassion and guidance. This chapter will outline some of the characteristics of adolescence; the influence of culture, age and maturity level on adolescent expressions of grief; and some characteristics of grieving teens.

The maturing adolescent student

Young people between the ages of 13 and 18 are no longer children. But even though they may look more and more like adults, they are still in the very complex and confusing process of developing physically, psychologically and emotionally.

Teens and adults

The teen years are a time of great change, emotional instability and uncertainty. The task of young people during these years is to become more independent of parents and teachers. As they mature, teens take on more and more responsibility for their own choices. They are busy constructing their own value and belief systems, which may differ from those of the important adults in their lives. That is why, at a time when students are most in need of adult models of integrity, openness, stability and calm resolve, they often rebel against these very models. This difficult period of upheaval can lead to conflict both at home and at school.

Teens and friends

At the same time, teens lean heavily on their friends for comfort and advice. Their peers are going through the same process and are seen as understanding better what they are feeling. Friends worry about each other and cheer each other on. Friends encourage each other and give advice about how to respond to painful feelings. But a grieving teen's friends may be deeply confused about life's many challenges and be uncomfortable in the face of serious grief. The counsel teens seek from their peers when faced with serious issues may be inadequate or non-existent.

Adolescence is a time of volatile, exaggerated emotions; high levels of social and academic stress; peer pressure; dating; joyful and painful romantic relationships; and growing self-defined identity. No wonder teenagers often seem frustrated, distracted and confused! Add the experience of a serious loss and the result is a recipe for emotional meltdown.

A personal story

When my father died, I was 21 and about to have a child. My brother was 14 and going through a very tumultuous teenage rebellion against just about everything. I remember how my aunts comforted me after my father's death, holding me while I cried bitter, uncontrollable tears. But what stands out most in my memory was that my brother never cried. He held it all in and became very silent. He looked more angry than sad, more hurt than alone. For days he responded only to my mother. He never let anyone know how he was feeling. When I asked him why, he said, "Dad didn't like it when I cried. Boys don't talk about how they're feeling — they just don't."

Sharron McKeever

Culture and the grieving teen

Our culture is where we feel most at home. Its ways are familiar to us. It has shaped and formed us into the person we are today through its customs, values, belief systems, language, symbols and practices.

Our ways of dealing with loss and grief are highly influenced by culture transmitted to us primarily from its institutions (family, church, politics, schools) and the media.

Family culture

The way we express emotional pain is a learned behaviour. When young children experience a loss, they will watch for emotional clues from their parents or siblings. The loss of a pet at the age of three can teach something about how to mourn a future loss, such as moving to a new town and school at the age of 14 and leaving old friends and familiar ways behind.

When it comes to a powerful experience like a death in the family, cultural and social mourning norms can guide grieving. Some cultures encourage outward emotional expressions such as crying, wailing, hugging others, or wearing black after the death of someone close. Other cultures consider outward expressions of sorrow or pain appropriate for females but not for males. In such a culture, adolescent boys may have a difficult time expressing their feelings.

Research has shown that the suppression of these emotions may lead to later emotional difficulties. Teachers can help guide grieving students into a healthy expression of their emotions when loss occurs.

Popular culture

Teachers are well aware of the influence of popular culture on teens. Like peers, popular culture exerts significant pressure on a teen's identity. The uncritical media presentation of casual sexual relationships, for example, both creates and supports a growing acceptance of such relationships among teens. Music and movies have changed the meaning of "hero" from someone who helps others at great personal cost to someone who is financially successful and popular. It should be no surprise that popular culture also influences how we grieve.

The influence of age and cognitive and emotional development

To get a better understanding of adolescent development, let us take a look at the sub-stages of adolescence.

Early adolescence

Children first enter adolescence full of concern about whether they will be accepted by others. They are usually self-conscious about their appearance, the way they walk, the way they laugh or the way they relate to their parents and teachers in front of their peers. They believe that others are watching and judging everything they say and do. Because they are insecure, they may not feel comfortable expressing grief. They may also be uncomfortable with, and not very interested in, someone else's loss unless it relates to something they themselves have experienced.

Middle adolescence

As adolescents mature, they go through a period when they feel indestructible. They believe they will live forever and will somehow be protected from any real harm, even if they face great danger. If they experience loss during this time, they may express their grief in unhealthy ways, such as alcohol or drug abuse, fast driving or physical fights. Sexual activity might also be used as a way to look for the comfort and support found in close and intimate relationships.

Late adolescence

As the ability to understand deeper relationships increases and as teens mature emotionally, they are able to understand another's point of view. Not only are they able to support others more effectively, but they are also more adult in their own grieving. They are very similar to adults in the way they understand loss and the way they approach the grieving process. However, their expressions of grief are often intense and dramatic. Often they lack the experience that brings about a mature expression of their feelings.

Many factors affect the adolescent maturation rate, such as age. (Cognitive and emotional development are linked to aging.) Life experiences, parenting practices, cultural expectations and personality also contribute to the journey toward mature adulthood. When an adolescent student experiences a serious loss, the first step you need to take is to assess where the grieving student is cognitively and emotionally. What is the student's understanding of this loss and the impact it will have? How free is the student to talk about feelings? What responses are being shown that can help you understand what is going on inside?

Emotional response of the grieving teen

Some losses are too much to comprehend. For this reason, some teens may not seem to be affected by their loss. They are in a state of denial. But as time passes, this denial will fade and the pain of the loss will rush in to meet them face to face. You can help students through this stage by giving them space and allowing them to grieve in their own time. Let them know that you are there for them if they want to talk, and leave it up to them to initiate a conversation.

Teenagers can be deeply affected by grief following the breakup of a relationship, their parents' separation or the death of someone close to them. All emotions and feelings, including those associated with loss and grief, are more intense at this age.

Response to loss may be intense and unpredictable, with sudden emotional outbursts. Teens may express their emotions through withdrawal, nervous laughter, violent bursts of rage, tears or depression.

Although their grief may be profound, many teens work very hard to hide it. They fear that expressing their grief will leave them vulnerable, so they find distractions to avoid grieving.

Some grieving teens will become very active. They may participate more in activities such as jogging, dancing to loud music, writing or reading poetry, shooting hoops or just going for long walks alone or with a close friend. These are healthy ways teens use to deal with the intense pain and confusion of grief.

Ways to offer support

The search for independence may prevent teens from seeking the support they need and want from parents and teachers. Adults may need to approach them first.

Teens will look for peer support and are often very successful at beginning the grieving process with their friends. But most teens are not able to provide the kind of support friends need when the loss is major and the grief is profound. Unless they themselves have experienced serious loss and grief, they may feel helpless and try to avoid talking about the loss with a grieving friend. Grieving students need adults to be appropriate models of grieving and to support them in this journey, but sometimes adults assume a teen is receiving all the support he or she needs from peers or others.

Teens often develop their own rituals and symbols to express their feelings. Working collegially to help each other deal with feelings of loss and pain is very helpful to the grieving teen.

Spiritual counselling is often needed. Teens may experience a spiritual crisis at a time of great loss. They may question their faith, wondering how a loving God could let this thing happen. School chaplains can be a good resource at this time.

Factors that can affect grieving teens

Many teens do not have a history of loss to draw on. They do not know what is expected of them in the face of loss, so they hide what they are feeling and try to act "normal." Unresolved grief from a previous experience of loss (e.g., divorce, death, neglect) may increase the impact of new losses.

Some teens may be expected to help other grieving family members or friends, thus postponing their own grief. Delaying, altering or preventing the grieving process can lead to psychological and emotional problems that last a long time, perhaps even throughout life.

The intensity of the emotions associated with a serious loss (from divorce or death, for example) can resurface when memories of the loss return. Triggers can include special occasions such as birthdays, annual celebrations or graduation, when the grieving teen realizes that the loved one is not there to share in these pivotal moments.

Some unhealthy responses

A loss can be even more devastating if relationships within the family are already fragile. Normal family arguments associated with adolescence can leave a grieving teen with unresolved conflicts that cause feelings of guilt. These feelings are also common for teens dealing with a death or divorce. Most teens need to tell their teacher how they are feeling. Your acceptance and support is important. In time, their guilt will subside and give way to other, more positive emotions.

Often a loss can leave a teen feeling alone. The family members and friends they normally turn to might also be grieving and be unable to offer the necessary support. Some teens turn to sexual activity to fill this need and to provide a distraction from their pain.

For many teens, emotional pain is very hard to endure for an extended period of time. Some will seek out drugs and alcohol to avoid feeling the pain. Such distractions prevent them from dealing with their loss and finding appropriate ways to grieve. This kind of behaviour makes the grieving process more complex and long-lasting, and keeps life-giving energy tied up with grief. Avoid being judgmental, but at the same time identify for them the destructive nature of these choices.

Anger is a very common emotion for people who are grieving. Significant losses can fill adolescents with a range of feelings, some of which they have never felt before. Some of these feelings are so intense, they create an incredible amount of pent-up energy unless they are expressed in some way. Teens will sometimes release this energy physically by throwing things, punching a wall, or screaming at parents, teachers and friends with little provocation. Although such activities are natural releases for anger, they can become dangerous. Someone could get hurt. Provide students with healthier options (see Chapter 4).

Conclusion

Teens who have suffered a loss often feel that their life is out of control. They do not have the skills or life experiences they need to work through the grief they are feeling. Teachers can be a great blessing to grieving students by providing the support and comfort they need at these devastating moments in their lives.

3

Journeying with the Grieving Teen

Your own grief history

When students experience pain and sorrow in their lives, it is not unusual for them to turn to a trusted teacher for comfort and support. One of the best ways to begin preparing yourself to help grieving students is to look at your own experiences of grief. Your own history can both give you strength and trigger a fresh wave of grief. Sometimes you, like the students, will need time and support to handle loss and grief.

A *personal story*

I will carry with me always the life-altering event that occurred one spring day at the secondary school where I was teaching. The senior girls' basketball team was practising for a big game when one of the girls fell to the floor and died. The whole school was in shock. For the rest of the day, students milled around in the hallways in a daze, some crying, all gathered in small groups, trying to make sense of what had happened. The school chaplain invited students to come to him in the chapel and the principal called in the crisis team from the board office. While teachers were trying to deal with emotional outbursts in their classrooms, little was done to support the teachers who were also deeply shattered by the event. At the end of the day, I went home to my family, numb and exhausted. I wondered how the girl's gym teacher was handling things. She had just come back to school that week after losing her father to cancer.

Sharron McKeever

We share this story for two reasons. First, it is impossible to know when loss will meet you face to face, either personally or through your students. Second, it is important for school communities to support everyone in times of grief. Journeying with students in their loss and pain can be one of the most difficult tasks a teacher will ever have to do. There are times when teachers may feel so fragile from loss and grief that they cannot properly help a student in pain. You need to understand and care for your own grief so that you will not be overwhelmed as you walk with your grieving students. Referring a student to another teacher or to a counsellor may be the best thing to do when you are dealing with your own loss.

Talking with a friend, colleague, pastor or counsellor about unresolved or ongoing personal difficulties in your life would help. If this is not possible, the following questions might be a useful guide for generating a personal inventory of your own grief experiences. This list is not exhaustive; considering these experiences may prompt you to think of others.

A personal inventory of grief

- What is the first significant loss you can remember?

- How did you learn about that loss?

- Did you feel left out? Did your family try to protect you from the reality even though you knew something was wrong?

- What feelings did you have?

- Were there questions you wanted to ask but didn't think you should?

- Was your family very private in terms of feelings?

- To whom, if anyone, did you express your feelings?

- If you visited a sick relative in the hospital, or attended a funeral, were you prepared ahead of time?

- What scared or worried you?

- What helped? What was unhelpful or hurtful?

- Did your teachers and classmates know your situation? How did you feel about them knowing?

- Did you feel that you or your family were being judged (often a common response to such issues as divorce, suicide or violent death)?

- Did anyone belittle your grief, especially if it was the death of a pet?

- Were you given ample time and support to adjust to your new reality?

Knowing your own history and recognizing what was difficult for you will help you to better support your grieving students.

Identifying the grieving student

Identifying grieving teens is not always easy. Because they do not want to draw attention to themselves in front of their peers, they may act as if nothing is wrong. If you are aware of a loss and approach the teen, don't be surprised if she or he refuses to talk. Teenagers, especially boys, are often uncomfortable talking about their feelings.

The adolescent search for self-identity is an essential part of growing up, but it can also create a barrier between teens and adults that prevents teens from approaching an adult for help with problems. Teens may feel that an adult will try to tell them what to do rather than listen to how they are feeling. Good counsellors begin by listening. It is unlikely that students will approach a teacher with whom they do not already have a relationship of trust and respect. Even then, teachers may need to initiate the discussion with the grieving student. If you are that teacher, look for the signs of emotional distress and be ready and willing to start the conversation.

Signs of adolescent grief

A grieving student may exhibit one or more of the following signs:

- unusually unkempt appearance;

- withdrawal from classmates, friends or adults;

- sudden displays of emotion (e.g., crying in class or leaving class without permission);

- profound emotional reactions (e.g., wide mood swings, anxiety attacks, chronic fatigue, irritability, anger, aggression, oppositional behaviour);

- testing limits;

- lack of concentration and attention;

- sharp drop in school performance;

- sudden and unexplained absences from school;

- extended depression marked by a loss of interest in favourite activities; listlessness, sadness;

- physical symptoms, including headaches, stomach aches, sleeping and eating disorders;

- frequent complaints of illness or pain that seem to lack any physical cause;

- feelings of helplessness and hopelessness;

- expressed guilt or humiliation over personal failure to prevent loss; and

- increase in risk-taking and self-destructive behaviour: careless driving, sexual experimentation, alcohol or drug abuse, self-mutilation, talk of suicide.

Approaching a grieving student

Sometimes you will know or suspect a student is grieving. What should you do if the student does not seek help directly?

- Listen carefully to what the teen is saying and watch for any unusual behaviour. This is how some teens initiate a conversation or get you to notice and be alone with them so they can talk.

- When parents or others have informed you about a loss, tell the student that you know about what has happened and are willing to listen.

- Make time for a teen who wants to talk. This can be difficult if you are approached during class. If it is not possible to talk right away and the student needs prompt attention, invite the student to speak with the school chaplain or guidance counsellor immediately and then see you after class when you are free to give your undivided attention.

Confidentiality

Students may not wish to let others know what is happening in their lives, so confidentiality is important. But some things cannot be kept secret. Before opening up a conversation, tell the student that if you learn about something that is harmful, dangerous or illegal, you are bound by law to tell someone else and get help. Never promise to keep a secret without explaining this first. Then ask if the student still wants to share with you. If the student says no, make sure he or she understands that there is an open invitation to come back at any time, and that you will periodically check back with him or her.

Always respect the student's right not to share the loss with classmates. When the situation does not require you to inform the principal, but you feel that the principal and other teachers could be of help, ask the student for permission to involve them. Explain that other adults at school can support the student, especially if you are away. Also, if the student happens to get into trouble, others may be more understanding if they know what is going on.

Explain that you will not tell parents or guardians what is shared, but that you will maintain communication with home so that everyone can work together through this time of grieving. Usually, students are glad that other adults are willing to help them.

When a student discloses a loss during class

Sometimes a student may blurt out the loss experience to the whole class, or reveal it during prayer time. If this happens, express your care and concern to the student and suggest a time when you can talk further.

Helping the grieving teen

The task of guiding students through the grieving process is not easy. You cannot protect them from the pain and sorrow of loss; you can only journey with them as they come to understand and accept what this loss means for them. There is no magic formula for helping grieving students, but here is some advice you might find helpful.

- *Provide an environment that is safe*: private, respectful, non-judgmental, caring.

- *When students want to talk, give them your undivided attention.* This will let them know both that they are important and that their grieving is important.

- *Listen for the underlying feelings they are expressing.* Many teens may not have the background to help them through the loss. This may be a whole new experience for them. They are not always able to express their loss clearly.

- *Allow students to react to loss in their own way.* If students express feelings of sorrow, hostility or guilt, reassure them that their intense feelings are a normal reaction.

- *Don't try to force a teen to talk about feelings.* Students who feel comfortable with you and believe you are willing to listen will talk when they are ready.

- *Support and encourage questioning and dialogue.* When a teen's world has been turned upside down by loss, it is normal for the big questions to surface: Why did God let this happen? Why should I bother trying? What did I do to deserve this? Encourage the student to find his or her own answers to these questions. What teens need most is to find outlets for their emotions.

- *Correct any misunderstandings students may have.* Answer factual questions with factual answers (e.g., "Your parents' decision to separate has not been caused by you, even though it has affected you.")

- *Avoid offering advice or trying to solve problems.* You cannot take away their pain or undo the loss. You can only help them work their way through the problem.

- *Watch for signs of unresolved past conflicts* that may be influencing their grief (e.g., an argument with their dad before he died). Feelings of guilt need to be addressed or they could undermine healthy integration of the loss.

- *Assure them of your support.* Students often feel helpless and overcome by their loss.

- *Help them focus on their strengths* and encourage constructive adaptive behaviour.

- *Assure students that it will take time to adjust to the loss.* Any loss represents a significant change. No two people respond to loss in the same way, and it may take one person longer to adjust than another. (Be sure not to impose your own timetable on their grief.)

- *Set boundaries for their behaviour.* Teens feel more secure if they understand what is expected of them.

- *Promptly attend to serious behavioural problems.* Discuss the inappropriateness of the behaviour with the student. If the behaviour persists, inform the principal and the student's family, and, if necessary, seek professional counselling for the student.

- *Encourage grieving teens to reach out to others.* Talking about a loss such as death or divorce can help students understand that they are not alone in their experience and that their feelings are normal. Telling their story provides them with a healthy expression of their emotions.

- *Invite them to join an appropriate support group* at your school or in your local community if you feel they would benefit.

- *Facilitate a discussion if grieving students wish to talk about their loss with their classmates.* If they do, begin by setting the tone of the discussion with the other students. Discuss the importance of confidentiality and respect for feelings. Remind students to listen attentively. Do not set a rigid timeline for the discussion. Listen for clues that will indicate when the discussion can be brought to an appropriate conclusion.

- *Do not expect grieving students to perform well academically.* Although they may not be able to concentrate on school work, it is still best for them to attend classes as usual. This offers them the comfort of routine and a sense of control in their lives. Give the student special concessions so they can still attain a sense of achievement (reduce homework, give extra time to complete graded assignments, allow them to listen rather than participate orally during class discussions).

Bringing in professional help

The support parents and teachers provide for grieving students is loving friendship and a shoulder to cry on. Some students may show signs that they need help from a professional to integrate their loss in a healthy way. The more complicated the loss and grief, the more students will need help that goes beyond what a teacher can offer. You may need to call in board staff or volunteers trained in grief counselling. For severely grief-stricken students, you may need to suggest to the parents intervention by a psychologist, psychiatrist, or family therapist who specializes in bereavement counselling.

Consider professional help if the student shows any of the following behaviours:

- talks about suicide or self-mutilates (you have a legal requirement to report this);

- is still unable to concentrate on any school work after several months;

- appears to be depressed or unhappy or cries a great deal of the time;

- has withdrawn from friends or has dropped out of extracurricular activities;

- is preoccupied with death; or

- practises dangerous activities (drives too fast, drinks excessively, uses drugs).

Conclusion

Teachers play a significant role in walking with students through grief. At times, they are the only constant in a shifting, scary world. Some students rely on teachers to care for them, let them express their feelings appropriately, and provide a haven of routine amid changing circumstances.

You live with your students for most of the day, and your relationship with them goes far deeper than simply delivering curriculum. Although you are not the only adult who supports them as they journey through loss and grief, you are a big part of their lives. You enter their world to stand with them and become part of their journey. Frightened, lonely, sad, angry, grieving students cannot learn.

Elizabeth Kübler-Ross has said, "If the desperate child has one human being who cares, one person who can hear the often non-verbal plea for help, a disaster can often be prevented."[1] In the words of Pope John Paul II, "Do not be afraid!" As time goes by, your students will not remember the things you said, but they will be strengthened by the gift of your time, attention and knowledge.

In her book *Children in Crisis*, educator Fran Newman challenges each of us to be there for our hurting children with these words: "If not you, who? If not now, when?"[2] This is truly holy work!

[1]   Cited in Fran Newman, *Children in Crisis* (Toronto: Scholastic, 1993), p. 204.
[2]   Ibid., p. 205.

4

Ongoing Support for Grieving Students

This chapter contains strategies for walking through the grieving process with your student or class.

What to do

- Be certain that the information students receive is accurate. Incorrect information can often add to the confusion of loss.

- Share honest feelings about the loss. If the loss is a death, share your own memories of the person, such as "I will always remember Ricky's amazing sense of humour, even when he was so sick in hospital."

- Always be truthful, even in your efforts to protect the students from sadness.

- Create a climate in which the students feel comfortable asking questions and know they will receive honest answers.

- Be honest and acknowledge you don't know when you do not know.

- Use correct terminology related to death. The person has died and is not just "gone away" or "asleep."

- Listen carefully so you can hear what students ask or say and not what you think they ought to ask or say.

- Bring a sensitive and caring attitude to the students' age-appropriate comments or grief responses.

- Allow students to express as many feelings as they are able or willing to share. Respect a range of responses, whether they involve quietness, questioning or emotional upset.

- Be sensitive to cultural differences in response to the loss. Help students become aware of culturally appropriate behaviour.

- Share your faith with the students to model an appropriate faith response. God loves us deeply and is with us in life and in death. God does not take someone to heaven because God needs another angel. God does not make natural catastrophes happen, and they are not a form of punishment. These occur as part of the unfolding way nature works.

- Involve the students as much as possible in tasks related to a remembrance or memorial ritual.

- Always respect a grieving student's wishes and share only the information he or she wants you to share with the class. When a family member is seriously ill or dying, some students may not want the whole class to know. You may want to spend time gently encouraging the student to give you permission to share this information so the class can offer support, be understanding and, as a community, pray for the person.

- Tell the student that you will share his or her loss with the principal and other staff persons who might be able to help them.

- When the loss requires that the school stay in contact with the family, identify one school spokesperson so the family will not be overwhelmed with phone calls.

- Always ask for support when you feel you need it.

What not to do

- *Don't* say something in an artificial way in an effort to sound positive, such as "Don't worry, moms and dads fight all the time. Everything will be fine." *Do* bring a sense of hope in God to the discussion. "Even in times of trouble, God is always with us."

- *Don't* link loss, suffering or death with guilt, punishment or sin. *Don't* blame God by offering false comfort statements. God does not need the person in heaven and does not cause us to suffer because we did something wrong. *Do* help students to see how God is with them through the caring of other people.

- *Don't* try to correct students' feelings or comments unless they share inaccurate information. *Do* help them find ways to express feelings through movement, play or art.

- *Don't* lecture. A crisis is not the time to make a point or moralize about the event. *Do* take time to pray as a class, aloud or in silence.

- *Don't* force students to take part in a discussion. *Do* encourage them to find someone to talk to if they are struggling.

- *Don't* process a loss endlessly. Routines may need to be altered, but not discarded completely. You may need to return to the discussion from time to time. *Do* offer activities such as writing letters, cards or journals to give the students' grieving a sense of direction and focus.

- *Don't* say, "I know how you feel." *Do* say, "I can't imagine what this must be like for you, but I care about you very much and I am here for you."

- *Don't* tell students how they are to feel. *Do* give them space to discover how they feel and ways to express it.

- *Don't* overload students with information. *Do* give sufficient information and wait for their questions.

- Don't feel you have to fix the sadness and hurting. Do support the students' right to grieve.

- Don't readily dismiss or discount a student's loss because it may seem minor to you as an adult (e.g., a love relationship that has broken up). Do help the student to cope with the loss and move forward.

- Don't take a whole class to the visitation at a funeral home. In preparation for some students visiting the funeral home with their families or close friends, discuss appropriate etiquette and the need to respect family members. Tell them that excessive displays of sorrow can be very upsetting for the family. If the class attends a funeral Mass, parents need to be informed and encouraged to attend the Mass also.

Suggestions for Specific Situations

When the home environment is in crisis

In the event of a miscarriage, help the student realize that this is a death and not to minimize it. It is important that the student knows that you are aware of the situation, you are watching out for him or her at school, and you are willing to talk.

In the event of a separation or divorce, some students will keep the information completely to themselves.

You may need to take steps to approach the student. If you know that a separation is occurring, arrange a time to speak privately with the student. Say that you are aware that his or her parents are separating and that this might be a difficult and confusing time. He or she may be comfortable talking further or may just be glad that you know. Tell the student you will provide opportunities to talk again. Do not leave this entirely up to the student – take the initiative even if it feels as if your caring has been rejected.

The disruption of moving

When a student is moving away, affirm her or his sadness and fears about missing school and friends and give positive encouragement about the new adventure. Providing e-mail addresses could be a good way to show that you wish to stay connected. This might help the student feel less fearful and bereft.

When a new student arrives, a warm welcome is essential. Pair the student with a couple of trustworthy buddies until he or she finds new friends. Offer opportunities for new students to share about their background. Checking in with them privately can provide needed reassurance.

Be particularly vigilant with students who come as immigrants or refugees. Be a mentor for these newcomers, and invite other teachers and students to do the same. The more support they have, the smoother the transition will be.

If your school happens to be near a women's shelter, some of your students may be in your class for only a few weeks because of the transitory nature of their lives. Welcome them and make them feel at home as much as possible.

Situations Involving the Whole Class

Sometimes situations occur that affect all of your students.

Personal Story

Some years ago, I was asked to help a teacher tell his class about a Halloween prank that had gone terribly wrong. One of his students had accidentally shot another classmate in the eye with a pellet gun.

The teacher was magnificent in his caring, his tears and his non-judgmental approach toward both the one harmed and the one responsible for the harm. He calmed the class's fears, answered questions, allowed them their feelings and, when the time was right, gently led them back to some semblance of routine. Although he was very capable and had great rapport with his students, he allowed them and me to see him when he was overwhelmed. He was a wise man in recognizing that there is strength, not shame, in being vulnerable. Teachers do not have to be rugged individualists!

Cathy Gross

Natural disasters such as flooding, tornado, fire or earthquake

In the past few years, we have experienced worldwide catastrophic events resulting in great loss. The following are examples of situations that can affect a whole class or school community and some suggestions for how to handle them.

When the disaster occurs in your region or involves your students' relatives, give students opportunities to tell their stories and give voice to their fears. Time for prayer, bulletin board displays, collages, scrapbooks, cards and letter-writing gives them something concrete to do so they do not feel helpless. With permission from the principal, a collection or small fund-raising project can give students a focus and a way to reach out and help.

When students see far-off disasters on television, they may be afraid that these can happen close to them. Teachers need to be appropriately reassuring. For example, instead of saying you will never have a flood even though you live near a major river, explain that emergency plans are in place and many people are specially trained to help and get people to safety ahead of time. Bringing in footage of people helping those affected by a natural disaster will help students focus on feelings of hope and caring.

Serious illness, accident or death of a classmate, sibling, teacher or other staff member

Your principal generally will take the lead in these cases. Ideally, your board has a Crisis Response Plan in place to provide guidance. This can be a very emotional time. It is all right to cry with your students, but it is critical to have another adult to help you share the information with your class as soon as possible. In some boards, a religion consultant can support you as you reach out to your students.

School lock-down due to crime in the neighbourhood

Students may experience feelings of terror when the school is locked down because of criminal activity in the area (a serious crime has been committed in the neighbourhood, or vandalism has been done to your school). Rely on your principal or a designated person to be the spokesperson for the school who will convey accurate information to the staff.

Try to prevent rumours from starting. Give your students the opportunity to put names on their feelings and to take control of their fears. If possible, when the time is right, invite a police officer to speak to the class. Reassure the students that they are safe.

Re-establishing routines

In all the above cases, it is important for students to return to normal routines after a reasonable time has been taken for discussion and related activities. Provide more individual support for students who are most affected. Deal with the loss again as a class at a later time as long as there is a need. It can be helpful and meaningful to mark the one-month, six-month and first-year anniversaries with a special prayer or prayer service so the students know that the loss is not forgotten.

Helpful strategies

As teachers, we can play an important role in helping students express their wants, needs and feelings through words rather than by acting out in negative or hurtful ways.

- Provide opportunities for music, poetry and art.

- Ask students to complete sentences such as
 – I feel like crying when…

– I feel sad when…
– I feel worried when…
– I am frightened that…
Assure them that all these feelings are normal. Everyone who has had a loss feels these kinds of feelings.

• Encourage students to use a journal to express their feelings openly.

• When a student has moved, is seriously ill or has died, have the class express its loss by creating a photo album or book of memories including poems, personal stories, photos, etc. This could be displayed in the school library or sent to the student who has moved or is ill. In the case of a death, it could be offered to the parents of the deceased student.

• The topics of divorce, abortion, death, rape and AIDS are part of the Family Life and Religion program. Be sensitive to the presence of students who may be experiencing related losses. You may need to postpone a particular lesson or structure it with the student in mind. It is always important to affirm God's grace and mercy when teaching these topics.

• In some cases, it might be appropriate to encourage the grieving student to share pictures and stories of the person who has moved away, is ill or has died.

• If the student talks about a dream she or he had about the loss, listen intently. Do not try to analyze the dream, but help the student understand that dreams are our mind's way of dealing with experiences that give rise to intense emotions.

• Writing a letter, even though they may not send it, is a safe and effective way for students to get in touch with their feelings. Speaking angry words, moving away and ending romantic relationships are all acts that result in broken relationships. In the case of death, a relationship is ended forever. Encourage the student to write a letter to the person to tell them how they feel. A letter may help the student to begin the process of reconciliation or to say goodbye.

Conclusion

This book highlights the importance and the need for prayer in dealing with the losses of our lives. Faith and hope in God's great love for us provide the foundation for meaningful prayer. When the loss is a death, ceremonies of remembrance bring healing.

In our prayer, we ask for God's guidance that we may grow in strength, hope and trust. When we are grieving, the future often feels and looks uncertain. Grieving is a long process; we need to be patient. There are no quick and easy solutions. As the Book of Ecclesiastes reminds us,

> *For everything there is a season,*
> *and a time for every matter under heaven:*
> *a time to be born, and a time to die…*
> *a time to weep, and a time to laugh;*
> *a time to mourn, and a time to dance…* (3.1 ff.)

New life that can emerge from life's losses will express both continuity and transformation. The caterpillar becomes a beautiful butterfly. The seed becomes a plant or flower. The egg becomes a chick. When Jesus rose from the dead, he was the same Jesus, but he was different. Even some of his disciples did not recognize him in his new life.

As your students move through the grieving process, they too will undergo great changes. With the grace of God and the help of caring teachers, they will emerge stronger in their understanding of life's sorrows and with increased empathy for all who experience loss.

PRAYERS FOR TIMES OF LOSS

This section contains prayers designed for students as well as a liturgy for the school or class.

When a student or staff member dies, it is customary for the teacher to tell the students and then to pray a brief prayer with them. A crisis team may be in the school to help staff and students cope with the loss. Late in the day, students gather to help create a personalized liturgy, which is usually celebrated within one or two days. If a priest is available, they could choose to celebrate a Mass.

Reflection – When something truly sad has happened

Use this prayer in a time of crisis, such as a death or serious illness, or in the face of terrible news events or natural disasters that students are concerned about.

Invite students to sit comfortably and quietly as you offer this prayer of reflection.

Sometimes we don't know how to pray.

At times like that, it helps to remember that the Spirit of God lives
    within us.
God knows us even better than we know ourselves.
God knows how we feel, even when we can't put our feelings into
    words.
The Spirit of God will help us in our sorrow.

No matter what happens, God wants to help us.
God gives us the strength to keep going.
God's love is stronger than sorrow and death.
God's love is forever.

I am sure that nothing can separate us from the love of God:
not hunger, not danger, not any other creature in the world,
not life, and not death.
Nothing can separate us from the love of God.

(Adapted from Romans 8:26-27, 38)

Play or sing "Be Not Afraid" (Isaiah 49) or another appropriate hymn.

Prayer in time of loss and suffering

Read Mark 4:35-41, below (Jesus calms the storm).

Tell students that Jesus has just spent the day healing the sick and telling thousands of people about God and God's great love for them. He is very tired and needs to rest.

On that day, when evening had come, he said to them, "Let us go across to the other side." And leaving the crowd behind, they took him with them in the boat, just as he was. Other boats were with him. A great windstorm arose, and the waves beat into the boat, so that the boat was already being swamped. But he was in the stern, asleep on the cushion; and they woke him up and said to him, "Teacher, do you not care that we are perishing?" He woke up and rebuked the wind, and said to the sea, "Peace! Be still!" Then the wind ceased, and there was a dead calm. He said to them, "Why are you afraid? Have you still no faith?" And they were filled with great awe and said to one another, "Who then is this, that even the wind and the sea obey him?" (Mark 4:35-41)

Reflection

All of us have storms in our lives. When we lose someone or something we really love, we may feel as if we are all alone, and that no one cares. But Jesus always cares. When the storm is too much for us, when our sorrows are too heavy for us to bear, he is there to calm the storm. Think about the storms in your life. Who was there to calm your fears? Who comforted you? Through the love of these people, Jesus came to you and offered to calm the waters. All he asks is that you have faith; that you continue to hope and know that he is present in those who love and support you.

Concluding prayer

> Faithful God, this is a difficult time for us. We need your help and the help of others. Give us the strength and courage to believe there is hope. We know you are with us in this time of worry and fear. Help us to recognize your presence. **Amen.**

Prayer – When someone we love dies

Loving Jesus,

Through your life, death and resurrection you taught us that God never abandons us.

You promised that we would share in God's gift of eternal life and happiness.

We believe.

Open your loving arms to receive _____,
who has died and awaits your welcome.

We know you are with us in our sorrow.

Help us to accept the pain that accompanies the loss of someone we love.

Help us to understand that we must die in order to live with you forever.

Like a seed that falls to the ground, we must die to our earthly bodies to be reborn with you.

Help us to accept this mystery of life in faith, for it is beyond our understanding.

Jesus, we trust that you are with us in our sorrow.

We thank you for your steadfast love.

We praise you, for you have overcome sadness and death forever.

Amen.

Psalm 27 (adapted)

Response: God is my light and my strength.

God is my light, helping me to see hope in my sorrow;
I shall not be afraid.
God is my source of strength;
I shall face my losses with courage.   R.

O God, hear my voice when I call out to you;
please have mercy on me and answer my prayers.
It is your face, O God, that I seek;
do not hide your face from me.   R.

I am sure I shall see God's goodness
in the land of the living.
Hope in God, be strong and have courage:
Hope in God!   R.

A blessing for those who grieve

May God hear you as you cry out in sorrow;
May God wipe away all your tears;
May you know God's love through those who comfort you;
May you feel God's arms around you in the hugs you receive from
    your friends and family;
May you hear God's voice in the prayers people pray for you;
And may God's joy fill your heart
    when others give you a reason to smile.

Prayer to follow the news of the death of a student or staff member

(Adapted from Psalm 62:1-2)

Merciful God, we turn to you now as we grieve the loss of our friend _____, whose (sudden) death has left us confused and full of sorrow.

Loving God, cradle us in your arms, be gracious to us and be present with us in our loss. You have fashioned us as your own; our names are written on the palm of your hand. Sustain us with your love. Help us to reach out to others who are also suffering this loss. We pray for _____'s family and friends, that you will comfort them. Gather our friend _____ in death and bring him/her into the everlasting peace of your eternal home.

Amen.

Prayer service for students when a death occurs

This service can be used as a school liturgy or can help you prepare for the celebration of a memorial Mass.

Introduction

Jesus told us that where two or more are gathered in his name, he is there with us. We trust that as we gather here today to pray for our friend/classmate _____, Jesus is with us. Let us be still for a moment and welcome Jesus into our midst. (*brief pause while students settle and become silent*)

Through his life, death and resurrection, Jesus shows us how to pray in times of sorrow and how to accept the sorrows of this life. He prayed for the courage to overcome his fear, and prayed to God in all times of need. He taught us to pray, too.

By his example, Christ is our light that overcomes the darkness of our sorrow. When we place our trust in him, he will take away our fear and guide us through the pain of our losses. He is our comfort and our strength. The light of Christ is our hope and our promise of new life.

Invite the assembly to stand and join in singing the hymn.

Hymn: (can be sung while lighting a candle)

> "Children of the Light" (*Come and See* catechetical program
> [Canadian Conference of Catholic Bishops]. Year 4, #12)
> *"You Are the Voice," "Christ, Be Our Light"* or
> *another appropriate hymn*

First Reading (Joshua 1:9)
A reading from the book of Joshua.

Be strong and courageous;
do not be frightened or dismayed,
for the Lord your God is with you wherever you go.

The word of the Lord.
Thanks be to God.

Responsorial Psalm (Psalm 84; adapted)
Response: O God, we thank you for your endless love.

How lovely is your home, O God.
My whole being wants to be with you.
My heart and lips sing for joy to you, O living God.   R.

Even the sparrow finds a home,
and the swallow, a nest for herself,
where she can lay her young before you.
Happy are those who live with you.
They will always sing your praise.   R.

Happy are the people who have you for a friend;
happy are they who feel strong because they trust in your ways.
You wipe away all sadness and fill their lives with joy.
They are strong and have no fear.   R.

Hear our prayer, O God.
Look upon the face of your friends.
I would rather spend one day with you
than a thousand with those who choose to do wrong.
Lord, you give light to our eyes and protect us from harm.
Blessed are those who hope and trust in you.   R.

Gospel Acclamation (sung) John 11:25-26

Alleluia (outside of Lent)

Praise to you, Lord, king of eternal glory (during Lent)

I am the resurrection and the life, says the Lord.
Those who believe in me will never die.

Gospel (John 14:1-3)

A reading from the holy gospel according to John.

Glory to you, Lord.

Jesus said to his disciples:
"Do not let your hearts be troubled.
Believe in God, believe also in me.
In my Father's house there are many dwelling places.
If it were not so, would I have told you that I go to prepare a place
    for you?
And if I go and prepare a place for you,
I will come again and will take you to myself,
so that where I am, there you may be also."

The gospel of the Lord.

Praise to you, Lord Jesus Christ.

General Intercessions

The response to each petition is: **O God, we know you are with us.**

For our friend _____, and for all those who
    care for him/her, we pray… R.

For all people who are suffering loss and seeking hope and comfort
    in your promise of resurrection and new life, we pray… R.

For those who have no hope, we pray…   R.

For the sad and the lonely, including ourselves, we pray…   R.

For all the quiet yearnings of our hearts, we pray…   R.

Presentation

If students have created cards or memory boxes in honour of the deceased, these could be brought up at this point and either laid on a prayer table or altar or given to a representative of the family.

Leader: Let us pray.

God has chosen you to be his hands in this world. Go now and be Christ to one another, be comfort for those who mourn, be hope to those in despair, be joy to those who weep. Go in peace in the name of the Father, and of the Son, and of the Holy Spirit.

Amen.

Closing hymn: "We Are Many Parts," "On Eagle's Wings" or another appropriate hymn.

Resources

In Grades 7 and 8, novel studies such as *Tuck Everlasting*, *The Outsiders* or *The Giver* lend themselves to discussion about loss. Selections from the English curriculum in high school also provide openings; Shakespeare's *Hamlet* or Emily Brontë's *Wuthering Heights* are just two examples. It is also possible to use picture books at this level, because the concepts can be accessed at any age. For example, Margaret Wise Brown's *The Runaway Bunny* (Harper Collins, 1972) beautifully illustrates how God, like a steadfast mother, will never abandon us.

Students may also choose clips from favourite movies or songs to explore the grieving process.

Resources for students

Buscaglia, Leo. *The Fall of Freddie the Leaf: A Story of Life for All Ages*. Toronto: Holt Rinehart and Winston, 1982. (As Freddie experiences the changing seasons along with the other leaves, he learns about the cycle of life/death/new life.)

Goble, Paul. *Beyond the Ridge*. New York: Bradbury Press, 1989. (A spiritual journey into the afterlife – beyond the ridge – as experienced through the death of a Plains Indian grandmother and her grieving loved ones.)

Gregory, Valiska. *Through the Mickle Woods*. New York: Little, Brown and Company, 1992. (After his wife's death, a grieving king journeys to an old bear's cave in the mickle woods, where he hears three stories that help him go on living.)

Grollman, Earl. *Straight Talk About Death for Teenagers: How to Cope with Losing Someone You Love*. Boston: Beacon Press, 1993. (A compassionate guide by an award-winning author that helps teenagers cope with grief. Contains a journal section.)

McLaughlin, Kirsten. *The Memory Box*. Omaha, NE: Centering Corporation, 2001. (A young boy, mourning the loss of his grandfather, fills a memory box with things that remind him of times they spent together.)

Mellonie, Bryan and Robert Ingpen. *Lifetimes*. New York: Bantam Books, 1983. (A helpful tool for explaining that death is part of life and that all living things reach the end of their own special lifetimes one day.)

Polacco, Patricia. *The Keeping Quilt*. New York: Simon and Schuster, 1989. (The Keeping Quilt, made from a family's old clothes, is passed along from mother to daughter for almost a century and becomes a symbol of enduring love and faith.)

Stoppard, Tom. *Rosencrantz and Guildenstern Are Dead*. New York: Grove/ Atlantic Inc., 1994. (Looks at *Hamlet* from the point of view of two minor characters who wander in and out of *Hamlet*'s plot, eventually finding a path of their own that will end in tragedy. Witty and endearing.)

Wood, Douglas. *Grandad's Prayers of the Earth*. Boston: Candlewick Publications, 2002. (Grandad explains how all things in the natural world pray and make a gift to the beauty of life, so when he dies his grandson finds comfort.)

Resources for adults

Cooper, Noel. *Language of the Heart: How to Read the Bible* (A User's Guide for Catholics). Ottawa: Novalis, 2003. (An award-winning, user-friendly introduction to the Bible. Offers language and explanations that help with understanding the concept of God-with-us in our losses rather than the cause of these losses.)

Fitzgerald, Helen. *The Grieving Child*. New York: Simon and Schuster, 1992. (Provides guidance for explaining death to a child, covering such areas as visiting the seriously ill or dying, difficult situations such as suicide and murder, attending a funeral, and the role of faith.)

Grollman, Rabbi Earl. *Bereaved Children and Teens: A Support Guide for Parents and Professionals*. Boston: Beacon Press, 1996. (A comprehensive guide to helping children and teens cope with the emotional, religious, social and physical effects of a loved one's death.)

Wezeman, Phyllis, Jude Dennis Fournier and Kenneth Wezeman. *Guiding Young Teens Through Life's Losses: Prayer, Rituals and Activities*. Mystic, CT: Twenty-Third Publications, 2003. (Covers such subjects as coping with the death of a parent or sibling, depression, alcoholism and drugs, and includes prayers and activities to comfort and strengthen young teens dealing with loss.)